Tears
of Eternity

by
Michael W. Hotaling Sr.

authorHOUSE™

1663 LIBERTY DRIVE, SUITE 200
BLOOMINGTON, INDIANA 47403
(800) 839-8640
WWW.AUTHORHOUSE.COM

First published by AuthorHouse 07/12/05

ISBN: 1-4208-4066-5 (sc)

Library of Congress Control Number: 2005904282

Printed in the United States of America
Bloomington, Indiana

This book is printed on acid-free paper.

Dedication

To my wife Jeannie, son Mike Jr., daughters Nicole and Kristan, granddaughters Chanel, Angelina, and Isabella and grandson Hayden, you are all my reasons for being. To all the guys that served in Hell and came home, Welcome Back. Most of all to those that gave their all, you are sorely missed.

May the words in these poems help others find that time and place they have been searching for, and to remember, you are not alone as we all have feelings, whether we are warriors, moms, dads, brothers or sisters, teachers, doctors or policemen.

Enjoy…

Contents

Tears
of Eternity

The Gates Of Hell
Just friends talking, remembering.

The Gates Of Hell

There we were all alone
Just four young men
Far away from home
Marking time in The Nam

The jungle around us
Seemed so very near
Closing in on us as we crept along
Not knowing where we were
But knowing where we belonged

It seemed like a bad dream
But we knew that it wasn't
So on we went, along this trail
That would lead us straight
To those great big gates of Hell

And then there he was
Our man in silk
That Airborn Jockey
Who had lost his wings

The heat was stifling, the bugs tenacious
As we worked on our wounded friend
His condition was as terrible
As his bulk was immense

Our High Cap was gone for now
But we were not alone
For not far away was the N.V.A
And those great big Gates Of Hell

Michael W. Hotaling Sr.

The race was on
Who would get the prize?
Our buddies aloft
Or Luke the Gook
The keeper of the jungle

The clatter of gunfire
The screeching of rockets
The flying debris, the clouds of smoke
The cries of pain, The devil closing in

The battle was intense
As our little buddies above
Made their mighty presence felt
And still the Devil came...

We were being welcomed by the Devil
At those Great Big Gates Of Hell
But to the Devils dismay
We were not to stay

For above us hovered our Guardian Angle
With all her little buddies
To extract us from the grasp of the Devil
And those Great Big Gates Of Hell

So off we went with our tattered prize
The winner this time
But who is to say...
To our dismay

Who the winner will be
The next time we go and play
In the Devils back yard
Near those Great Big Gates Of Hell

By:MICHAEL HOTALING,1980

1968

I was listening to the radio on a Saturday night and they were featuring the year 1968. They kept playing songs that I couldn't remember, and it just hit me.

1968

1968, Where did it go
I went away to a foreign affair
I lived out my time to the fullest
But when I came back...
1968 was, and went, but I don't know where

I spent my year away from here
1968 lived, but I missed it here
Oh I lived my year, like many of us
In that far away land-The Nam
I can relate to my 1968, Ah yes but you can't

You pointed the fingers, and spat on us
You shouted those words, but you kept your distance
The music came and went, and I didn't know
You took life day by day, and song by song
I took life minute by minute, and second by second

You took your freedom, and I earned mine
1968, the year that came and went
And that's as far as I got in it
I came back, a stranger in my own Home Town
1968, where did you go.

Tet came and dominated early on
Operation Game Warden, Sea Dragon Ops, 1968 lingered on
And yet back in the world, I don't remember
But 1968, I do remember, for I endured, survived..
But back in the World....I don't remember-

01/30/04

TONY

Tony and I went through high, school together. We drove to the Oakland induction center in Oakland in 1967, and flew down to San Diego to Boot Camp together. Our last words to each other were " keep your head down, don't be a hero." My first day back, I found out that Tony was killed on Easter Sunday, 1968.

TONY

Together we played
Together we excelled
You In gymnastics, me in tennis
And then came that call
You The Marines
Me The Navy

Together we went to The Nam
So innocent, so confident
So full of pride
My tour was over, and back to the world
And then came the news....that One had fallen
And all I could think of was my buddy Tony

We both made it back
But for you it was permanent
And so unfortunate
And for me, I thought I was so lucky
Khe Sanh, Hue, Tet 1968
We endured all, but only one survived

The pain so deep, The sorrow still lingers
19 years later I said my good-by
You were my shadow for so very long
And I laid you to rest on the other side of time.
Easter Sunday 1989
But, you are with me still, and always will be.
Dark flashing eyes, that quick knowing smile,
And still so very young with the heart of a lion
I'll never forget you, Semper Fi.
For you are my buddy, Tony.

By:Michael W Hotaling, 1989

Tears of Eternity

Every time I hear that another one of our guys has been
killed somewhere in this world, I get tears in my eyes. The
pain is still there.

Tears of Eternity

As the years passed on, not a tear appeared, nor was a word
ever uttered.

Of that land so far away but yet, in my every thought forever
and a day.

Then one day ten years removed, a tear appeared that would
not be denied.

The words started to flow and I was going to be heard.

I think of Tony, Steve, Don and Ken, all so young, and still
so very young.

I see their faces, somber and dark and my tears start to slide
down my cheek.

Ten years of holding back the flow has had its price.

At first the words were all in a jumble, in a hurry to be heard.

The memories so fresh, just like yesterday, but ten years had
gone.

The pain was still there like it always has, as will the sounds
of their voices.

The stench of that humid piece of jungle that still holds their
last breath.

I will never forget, and will forever shed a tear when another
passes on.

Thirty-four years have passed and still the tears flow
As I watch the evening news I learn another warrior has
    fallen.
Passing on through to the other side. A brave man in
    another far away war.
His mission was just, his heroism true. And his sacrifice was
    supreme.
He too will stay forever young, just as all those that passed
    before him.
Every time I hear from the past I think of Tony and the
    others.
Their faces still so somber and dark, the tears continue to
    flow.

I know as many of us do that these tears will continue for an
    eternity
As will those words we held so close for those foreboding ten
    years.
Our pain will continue to surface, every time those images of
    the long gone past.
Flow past our eyes with the faces of Tony, Steve, Don and
    Ken.
Still so somber, dark and forever young.
I too one day will cross over to the other side and join my
    fellow fallen warriors.
And it will be time for someone else to shed those tears of
    eternity.

Mike Hotaling
Nov 11, 2002

Why
Just because....

Why

The pain is still there from so long ago
At least once a day my thoughts flow back
To that time and place that won't let go
I still see the faces, the sounds so real
The smells are imbedded in my senses forever
There is no shaking that feeling of pain and fear
And I still ask myself that same old question....Why

Not a day goes by that I don't make that trip
I don't have a trigger to caress, a trip wire to find
It's the moment when the tide comes in, and finely recedes
And that tear starts to form at the corner of my eye
The wind charges and I catch a smell, nothing else.
My hair stands on end, but I continue my day
And once again I ask myself. Why....

I hear that sound of the screeching jet engines, the fireworks
    go off
The crowd at the park goes wild with enjoyment and...
My mind starts to swim; my insides turn to jello, Like a giant
    blender
My eyes search for a corner, but I maintain my control
The fans at the park are cheering the show, unaware of my
    internal strife
And once again I ask myself that age-old question......why

My energy leaves me, my head is swimming, my pulse is
    surging
My center is tumbling, but I maintain my control,
And another day has come and gone.
And that nagging question still lingers, and still I don't know
    why.

Michael W Hotaling Sr.
06/15/02

Never Again

One night at work it started to flow, I just put it to paper in about 20 minutes. I was pissed off at the Government, and out it came.

Never Again

The bitterness increases as time goes by
The distrust is there like never before
We are proud of the jobs we did
In that far away Hell that wont forgive

But one thing is for sure and that we swear
Our sons will never go to a foreign affair
That they did not want or did not declare
For they will not help line
Those heavy pockets of slime

Let the elite despair, with all of their money
Fight their own wars, and protect their own pots
For we shall see where their values lie
For they won't give their lives for their so called allies
Slime has no backbone like that of a man

Beware of that mad man dressed like a clown
For he will demand that you don't let him down
When in actual fact he wants you to die
Just so he can live, get rich, fat, and survive

As he sits in his castle, Persian rug beneath
Drinking his Colombian coffee, smoking his Hawaiian weed
Havana cigar, Russian caviar
As he watches you die on the six o'clock news
Without even batting an eye

So remember my friend, and you'll do yourself well
Believe nothing what you hear, and half of what you see
And you'll live a lot longer, and without so much anger
The peace from within will get you by the danger

Michael W. Hotaling Sr.

And let those who want, but not out of need
Do for themselves, to satisfy their greed
For they say we lost once before, through no fault of our own
But we shall never again play at a foreign affair

For he that wants just out of greed
Shall have to go and do his own fighting
And then he will know what it is to bleed
And then he too will say..Never again

By:Mike Hotaling..1982

Heads or tail

Sitting around a fire up at the lake, a night sky full of stars above, and the mind just took that trip back to a night in a far away land.

Heads or Tail

Victor-Charlie, Luc the Gook
Five foot nothing, tough as nails
Black pajamas, Conical hat
Watch him bob as he tricky trots down the trail
AK 47 on his shoulder, his rice ball in his bag

Eyes that dart from side to side as he approaches the point of
    no return
His singsong voice carries on the wind
The stench of Nuk Mam on his breath
Farmer by day, Killer by night
As he approaches his departure point,
his moment of truth.

He fills your cross hairs, you caress the trigger
And another one passes on; he'll never know-
Today, you win, tomorrow…..Who knows?
Better to be good and a little lucky, instead of just luck.

Michael W Hotaling Sr
07/20/1978

The Illusion

I wrote this poem to my son and his buddies when they were little boys. They used to play Guns in the creek behind our home. Little did I know at that time that they were to go off together, and spend a year in Iraq with the US Army, in the same unit. They all came back.

The Illusion

War is hell
It ain't a game
The bullets are real
And so is the pain

You lay your life on the line
Your comrades get hurt
And some even die
And like I said, It ain't a game

You talk about the good times
And you smile as you tell
But you can't shake the bad times
Even the smells
And like I said, It ain't a game

The blood is real
So are the cries
Your heart is pounding
Your throat is dry

The noise is intense, the action fierce
Beyond your wildest dreams
Yet everything is moving
Like a lazy summer stream

The next thing you know
You are now alone
Just the darkness of your room
And that private hell of the past
War ain't a game, it's really a hell

Michael W. Hotaling Sr.

Young boy, play your games
But remember it's an illusion
Games are fun to play
But war is really hell

By:MICHAEL HOTALING 1983

IMPLOSION
A breakup.. life goes on.

IMPLOSION

Everything I touched I destroyed
Everything I tried to hold I broke
My love for life has been destructive
My want for belonging was so desperate
And all I did was take it and break it

I never knew what love was about
I could only love the way I knew
I cared so much, but couldn't express it to you
I was living a hell, like a trapped animal
I just wanted to be loved, and couldn't

You gave me your love, and all your care
But I didn't know it, nor understood it
You gave me your support, and I rejected it
Everything you did I threw away

The pain is intense as I have found
My heart is heavy with sadness
My mind is confused, Where am I, What am I
I need help, but I'm afraid to seek, Why?

By:MICHAEL HOTALING 1986

REALITY

A Brief period of being unemployed, angry and down but not out, I continued on with life.

REALITY

The heavens are dark
The days are long
The hours trickle by
But there is no song

Hope, faith and charity
A line that has no meaning
For they are but an illusion
And now it's time for reality

It's all around, yet it is no where
It's everywhere, and yet I can't see it
Just reach out and touch it
Apathy, loneliness, just reality

They walk along, but not alone
They look for help, but it's not there
It's dangled out there, like a carrot
Read this, sign that, just like a dog

Do you rate, do you merit?
We have all paid our dues
We have all made our own way

Now we have stumbled
Fallen on hard times
And there it is again
Apathy, loneliness, and just reality.

By:Michael Hotaling
June 1986

TRIAGE

My mother was a Red Cross ambulance driver and nurse during WWII, we were sitting in her living room discussing casualties when the word struck that chord and I just wrote this poem in a couple of minutes.

TRIAGE

Twisted limbs, shattered minds
Destroyed visions of peaceful times
The future looks grim from this perspective
Life goes on for those who are willing

One step at a time, no matter how trying
You keep your head high, for you have your pride
Your time in hell has changed you forever
Your eyes don't lie, they still show the terror

A young man you went, dejected you returned
Your friends rejected you, a recluse you became
Withdrawing from their lives
Into your Nightmare of strife
Your private hell, your personal triage
Courage my friend, for I have been there.....

Mike Hotaling 1974

Shadows

My first night was spent under the dangeling lights of flares, I will never forget that eerie sight and sound.

Shadows

The sound of those words in your handset, "Shot out" and
   you wait for that light.
Pop, Pop, Pop, and the flares appear, suspended above the
   valley floor.
The silence is deafening, as the darkened landscape suddenly
   appears painted in that moon glow greenish yellow.
As the flares dangle beneath their silken chutes, dancing in
   the breeze with every breath.

The shadows jerking with every puff of wind, your eyes
   straining in dismay at the sight before you.
That alien landscape, and the questions arise.
Did that bush move…, was that tree walking…did you hear
   that scraping sound. Will the sun come up?
You hunker down closer to the ground, looking over your
   team, knowing that they too have those thoughts.
The shadows become longer as the flares get closer to the
   ground, and before you know it, you are enveloped
   under that stiffeling carpet of darkness.

The sounds appear louder, as your eyes strain to see, your
   heart jumps into your head,
The pounding, so loud, you know the others can hear, and so
   can Charles as he closes the distance.
Pop, Pop, Pop…go the flares, and that moonscape appears
   again with a jolt, just the shadows dancing.
Did that bush move, was that tree walking, was that a
   scraping sound in front of me.
Your hands tighten around the clacker, waiting to set off the
   monster strung out in front…
And once again fade to darkness, and the cycle begins again.

First light arrives, you think to yourself, I have survived, but
    another piece of my sanity has been lost.
The question comes again. "Will the shadow get me, will I
    survive".
You set security and pull in your claymores, moving out
    for the day knowing that another 64 dances with the
    shadows await you, as you work your way thru your full
    365.
You know you can do it, you and your team, for you have
    heart, and the will to survive.
So on you go with your dance card in hand, and only
    another 64 punches, and you will have won….

But will the mind follow, for the shadow is still there,
    beckoning you along, with Charlie in the middle
    whispering his song, as you watch the shadows, and
    listen for that sound… that chips at your sanity.
You are still there, but you wonder for how long, as you look
    at your dance card, and count your punches.
Your 365 will come, will you be there…? Or will only your
    shadow show with another 64 still to go….

Your alarm goes off and you reach to silence it   You stagger
    for the shower, hit the lights and one goes pop, And
    your face in the mirror stares back at you…am I really
    there…or back in the world…
Your dance card in hand..or is it… your eyes come into
    focus… You have survived.
But you know, that from time to time you will have to fight
    those shadows, and check your punch card
And only then will you know you have arrived. Pop, pop,
    pop…key your handset once and continue on.

By:Mike Hotaling
June, 2002

SHORT
When your short, your short.

SHORT

You survived once before, and you will once again
You'll search out for eyes with that same thousand meter stare
One thousand meters of darkness in front of your lair
And Charlie doing his dance of death beyond your line of
    sight
You sense his smile as you try and penetrate the darkness
Your mind plays games with your eyes and ears
And another piece of sanity is gone As your circuits become
    frayed
Your motions are short and quick as you react to that clock
Only 25 and a wakeup, and that brings a smile
I know I'm going to make it
Five, four, three, two, one, and then I'm gone...
Lookout world, here I come...SHORT!!!

Mike Hotaling 1976

SEARCH FOR TRANQUILLITY

Another bad night with the demons, sure makes for a long day.

SEARCH FOR TRANQUILLITY

You're more alive when you are lost
Then when you know where you are
Your senses are peaked as you search for your spot
That little place you call inner peace

Your heart pounds, your ears search out
Your hands reach out thru the darkness
As your eyes widen in anticipation
Where am I, What am I, Who am I

I know I'm alive because of the pain
My heart is pounding, and my ears ringing
My fingers are tingling, and my eyes are straining
I'm lost, but by god I know I'm alive

Please, help me find myself
For I'm tired of being lost
My head is swimming from all the searching
I know I'm live, but life must go on

I know one day I'll stop this lurching
Stop and go, Ups and downs, Ins and outs
I'll know when I'll have found my inner peace
For the pain will have gone,
Tranquillity will abound

By:MICHAEL HOTALING 1985

The long silence

When I came back, no one wanted to hear, so I didn't talk
about it for 10 years and a day.
That's how this book came about.

The long silence...

There they go again
The look of doubt
That look that says, Bullshit..
They ask you how it was
And then they laugh...
Bullshit they say, with a sly smile

What a line of shit...
They don't believe you
"No way man,It couldn't have been
A dream like that...you've got to be kidding"
That's what they say
They just stare and shake their heads

But then again, They weren't there
And that's why the long silence
The ten years of internal turmoil put to rest
Doubt me if you must, but you remember
You asked the questions, not I
It wasn't a picnic, no resort, no party
Just the way it sounds, just like a bad dream
As unbelievable as it may seem
Yes we did survive, a living hell that it was

So don't tell us about the bullshit
For we were there and you were....
We want no sympathy, just your respect
After ten years of silence, I will be heard
For if you were to ask the questions, I will answer
And make no mistake, a picture I will paint
As grim as it may seem, there won't be any shit
So respect my words, and me for having been
For I was there and you will never know....

Mike Hotaling 1981

That fog

Too many rules, too much ambiguity, just do it, handle it.

That fog

Black or White, It's so clear
Dead or alive, no in between
Back in the World there is so much gray
Which way to turn in this thick fog
It feels like an endless tunnel
With no light at the end

Being back in the World is not the same
Your friends look at you
As if you were a stray
And they don't understand
And they don't want to know
And here comes that sea of gray again

Those swells toss you and turn you
No matter where you go
They all seem to know
You just got back from the Nam
That living purgatory on earth
Where everything is confusing
But still Black or White

When something comes up
Back in the World
The gray seems to close
And put everything in a swirl
You cry out for help
And they just stare

Michael W. Hotaling Sr.

So you handle it yourself
And they all run from you
You hear the whispers
And you know those words
He's been to Nam
And he's come back a user

How little they know
And how little they care
If only they had asked
And had wanted to hear
That thick gray fog that envelopes
Would be gone by now

But it seems to follow
No matter where you go
The only time you know
Where and what you are
Is when you are alone
just you and your thoughts

Where everything is Black or White
Where only you know
If you are Dead or Alive
It's all from within
And no one cares

So on you stumble
Down that endless gray tunnel
You smile to yourself
For only you know
What it's like to live
Whether it's Black or White
Or a little Gray

By:Mike Hotaling/1983

Tedium 365

A One year tour for a friend of mine.

Tedium 365

The boredom let me tell you
You CA into a cold LZ
Then you hump the fingers and draws
And before you know it, last light is upon you

You set up your Night Defensive Position
And then you wait…and the rains come
The mosquitoes from above
The leaches from beneath

Your eyes seek out, your ears are peaked
You're wet and cold, you skin starts to crawl
You toss down your C's, cold that they are
As you set in for the night….

Waiting and waiting, knowing that Charles is there
And then at last …First light of false dawn
As you look around and see those eyes
That look of surviving, that Thousand meter stare

The tedium of the night has left you drained
And yet another day is about to unfold
More fingers, more draws, and more ghosts….
And the tedium of the day has set in again.

A terrific force and momentary disorientation
The ringing in the ears, dirt in the eyes
And then the cries, that searing pain
The sudden realization of that dreaded moment
…..Ambush…….

You react within a millisecond, the firing is intense
The concussions unreal, everything is moving so slow
And then that silence, and the action is over
Dust-off coming in, low and fast
You pop smoke, and evac is gone

There you are a couple of guys light
Names you don't remember, and the tedium continues
No glamour, no applause
Nothing but silence, the ringing in your ears
Endless boredom and terror sprinkled with mad minutes
And that terrible feeling of despair

I must survive my tour 365
And before I know it, I'm a single didget midget
Ready for my freedom bird back to the world
Short.........

Michael W. Hotaling Sr.

STRANGERS

Coni, A long distance relationship.

STRANGERS

The voice on the other end, so soft, gentle
Expectations that run a little high
No face to put to the voice on the end of the line
But her voice is intriguing, excitement abounds
We speak of our interests, probe for some clews
Our ages, color of hair, likes and dislikes
Not to fast, too bold or awkward, just right
There is that voice, soft and gentle, the face...
Over here, maybe there, who knows where
One day we shal meet, and who knows then...
And when we do, we will be able
To put a face along side of that voice
Soft, kind and with that gentle touch
No longer strangers, but friends in the end..

By:Michael W Hotaling SR..1990

I am the pond

I wrote this poem to my wife Jeannie, my savior in this world.

I am the pond

When I look into your eyes
You send a ripple accross my pond
As I watch you approach from afar
And once again a pebble is cast into the middle
And another ripple radiates accross my pond

Every time our hands touch, the pebbles start to fall
And as our lips come closer the land slides begin
You are such a joy to be around
Your touch, so soft, so caring
Your kisses so tender, so full of passion

No better place to drownd in your arms
As those ripples become waves of joy
I try to keep my head as your inner warmth consumes me
My pond has become a joyous sea of love

My darling, you are the only one to be
The only one to cast her pebbles into my sea
The sea that is realy my inner pond, ME
I love you my one and only pebble.

My friend
To a friend who's father "The Eagle" survived being in country, to later die from Agent orange.

My Friend

Your eyes so dark, so wide and full of life
Your lips so soft, your kisses so deep and full of passion
The feel of your touch so soft, tender, so caring
Your fragrance so fresh and wonderful, flavorful
You are quite a lady, so wonderful to be with

You have a way about you, careful and guarded
Yet you let me in, as your friend, I thank you
I move with care, understanding, for I have been there
My care for you is very strong, but I move within slowly
I am here for you, no matter where you may be

You are so good, right there....so strong, yet scared
Your past has left its marks inside of you
But have no fear, you are past them, and not alone
For I'll be there for you, no strings attached
You are my friend, like no other friend on earth

At times you wonder where you get your strength
For he is still there, that giant of a man
And for you he will always be, as in the past
When you were a little girl, and now as a grown woman
His spirit has never left, not even you could change that

The eagle is aloft, every day and night
And I am here for you, as I too understand
I too have walked down that same dark path,
My care for you is that of a special friend, always
And what comes our way, will come our way
But, no matter what...remember
I will always be first of all, your good friend

I love you...............

Michael Hotaling..1988

Dreaming

Somewhere on a beach, letting my mind wander…can be delicious.

Dreaming

The moon was bright
As she walked along the sand
And the closer she came
The better the sight

There she was on this moonlit night
Her body shimmering in this magic light
As she danced her way along the sand
Dancing to the music of an imaginary band

Oh my god was she a sight
That beautiful swing was like a wave
The closer she came
The louder my heart pounded

And then, there she was
Almost within my reach
Just her and me
Alone on this beach

I reached out to bring her close
And then she vanished into thin air
Just like a dream
And all I said was "It's just not fair"

So on I went
Into the bright moonlight
Looking for my next dream
To carry me through this long, dark night

By:Michael Hotaling 1981

Angelina

One of my grand daughters. We are so fortunate, as we see them all every week.

Angelina

That smile, so big, so quick
That laugh, so wild, so loud
The look of an angel, but the devil in her eyes
Angelena, you little sweetie
You're little feet pitter patter down the hall
Nona, Nona, you holler as you wander down with that smile
    in your eyes
Then you see me, hiding in the corner and you charge.
Grandpapa, you chortle as you lean into the surge, with your
    arms flailing
Your voice increasing in pitch as you get closer and dive into
    my arms.
You are what it is all about. That love of life,
That enjoyment of sheer delight and pure innocence
For you are my little granddaughter.

Mike Hotaling Sr
01/05/2002

Demons in the Night

A rough time that used to be a nightly visit that now rarely shows up.

1995
Demons in the Night

For a period of three weeks in 1995 I was having some very long nights, by myself, unable to put 2-3 hours of sleep together let alone a good few minutes of inner calm. I was waking up in a pool of sweat, short of breath and shaking badly.

I was dying, no doubt about it, I was dying. I couldn't take in any precious air deep into my lungs. There was a ten-ton demon standing on my chest and there was no way to move him off.

I would wake up in a pool of sweat, gasping for air, looking around to see where I was...Yup, there I was, in my own bed, next to my wife, but yet my body was somewhere else and dying.

I'd get up and sneak out of the bedroom, go into the garage and start doing jumping jacks, sit-ups, anything to force oxygen into my burning lungs. I was dying, but yet I knew there was nothing wrong with me physically.

There I was 0330, in total darkness, on my lounger, mentally checking myself out. No cold, No heart problems, not overweight, working out 3-4 times a week, and playing in the Friday night soft ball league, but here I was, dying.

I would sneak back into bed, look at my wife, sleeping Peacefully, and I would try to get back to sleep.

One hour later, I'm dying again. The sweat is pouring off me. I feel myself shaking, I see the flashes, hear the gunfire but there is nothing clear. No faces, no features. The smells are there, and the fear is there. The smell of death lingers in my nostrils, and I am dying all over again.

This has been a nightly trip for me for the past three weeks, and yet I can find no rhyme or reason for this. Monday morning, three weeks later rolls around, I'm in my office, and like a bolt of lightning it strikes me!

The bombing in Oklahoma, Robert McNamara's startling

revelation. "He was wrong, we should have never been there" The Nam... The 20th anniversary of the end of the War in Vietnam, For Whom?

There has never been an end, as much as I want to believe It.. Never! That came back to me clearly.

Now lets think about the thousands of other Combat Vet's who have been dealing with these Demons every day and night since the day they left that god forsaken country.

The Nam lives on in their memories. Is it over for them? No way, but they sure as hell wish it were over, But...

The Demons still take their nightly ghostly trips around the deep recesses of their minds. The man still looks for the key to unlock the door to let these maddening Demons out.

I am one of the fortunate one's; I don't fight these Demons on a nightly basis. I don't have to call in a nightly sit-rep that includes another piece of my mind crumbling off and disappearing into that abyss. I don't need a flare ship circling overhead dropping flares every couple of minutes until first light.

I pray for my fellow brothers, that they too will one day walk out of the Valley of Death and be able to smell the sweet fragrance of their loved ones, feel the warmth of the sun on their skin, and take that deep breath of fresh air all the way down to the bottom for their lungs, and be alive again, released from the grip of those Demons.

I hope this will help some poor soul somewhere out there pass on through to the other side. Back to the world.

May God bless and guide you.

> CHARLIE MIKE...
> (Continue mission)
>
> Mike Hotaling Sr
> Vietnam Veteran
> 1967-1968/1969-1970

About the Author

Michael W. Hotaling is a veteran of two tours of duty in Viet Nam with the U.S Navy. Serving in 1967-68 and 1969-70. After his discharge in 1971, Michael was attached to the Naval Special Warfare Group I, Special Boat Unit 11 at Mare Island California, off and on over the following 15 years, in a reserve capacity as a crew member on PBR's.

He has spent the last 20 years as a business consultant in hospital and medical clinics all over the West Coast, from Monterey to Alaska.

He now resides in the San Francisco Bay area with his wife Jeannie. He has a son who just completed a 1 year tour of duty in Iraq, two daughters, a grand son and 3 grand daughters. He works for a College in the East Bay Hills and spends his spare time coaching his Grand daughters in Soccer and Softball, fishing on his boat, and busies himself in his work shop at home. No project is too big.

Michael is currently working on his autobiography from his youth, growing up all over Europe, Asia and Africa.